the
greatness
principle

the greatness principle

FINDING SIGNIFICANCE AND JOY
BY SERVING OTHERS

nelson searcy

WITH JENNIFER DYKES HENSON

BakerBooks

a division of Baker Publishing Group
Grand Rapids, Michigan

© 2012 by Nelson Searcy

Published by Baker Books
a division of Baker Publishing Group
P.O. Box 6287, Grand Rapids, MI 49516-6287
www.bakerbooks.com

Printed in the United States of America

Library of Congress Cataloging-in-Publication Data
Searcy, Nelson.
   The greatness principle : finding significance and joy by serving
  others / Nelson Searcy, with Jennifer Dykes Henson.
     p. cm.
   Includes bibliographical references.
   ISBN 978-0-8010-1466-6 (pbk.)
   1. Christian life. 2. Service (Theology). 3. Self-actualization (Psychology)—Religious aspects—Christianity. 4. Success—Religious
  aspects—Christianity. I. Henson, Jennifer Dykes. II. Title.
  BV4520.S425 2012
  248.4—dc23   2012022182

The internet addresses, email addresses, and phone numbers in this book
are accurate at the time of publication. They are provided as a resource.
Baker Publishing Group does not endorse them or vouch for their content
or permanence.

12   13   14   15   16   17   18   7   6   5   4   3   2   1

To the members and regular attenders
of The Journey Church in Boca Raton, Florida.
Thank you for living out The Greatness Principle.

contents

prologue

the longing within

I bet I know what you want out of life. You may wonder how that's possible since we've likely never had a conversation. How could I know anything about you? How could I possibly presume to know what you want? Here's how I know: what you want is the same thing I want. It's the same thing my brother wants and the same thing your neighbor wants. It's the same thing gap-toothed elementary school kids and silver-haired seniors want. Deep inside each of us, there is a longing, a yearning . . . for greatness.

Greatness. Purpose. Significance. Impact. However we nuance it, the simple fact is that we all want to matter. We want to know that the world is different because we have lived. We have an innate need to make our mark and make sure we are remembered for something beyond average, something great.

This longing is nothing new. As far back as Jesus's day, his disciples argued with each other about who would be greatest among them (Luke 9:46). Their debate wasn't surprising, but Jesus's response was. He didn't tell them that they shouldn't want to be great. He knew it was a God-given desire. Instead, as he was often apt to do, Jesus reframed the discussion. Actually, he reframed the entire concept of significance. Jesus used the disciples' debate as an opportunity to fill them in on the secret of true greatness.

In the pages ahead, we are going to discover the secret to greatness that Jesus shared with his disciples. But before we even get started, let me give you some incredible news: you can be great. You can matter. You can find the purpose and significance you are longing for.

Greatness is possible and it is within your grasp.

1

discovering true greatness

It's not what you take but what you leave behind that
defines greatness.

Edward Gardner

What if you opened the newspaper tomorrow
morning and saw your own obituary? Would it
make you reevaluate your life? Cause you to reconsider
how you spend your hours? That is exactly what happened to Swedish inventor and chemist Alfred Nobel.
Alfred was the man responsible for inventing dynamite.
Even though dynamite is now synonymous with de-
struction, Alfred's original intent for the invention was
that it would save lives. He wanted to create something

so powerful that people would recoil from the thought of going to war with each other, thereby creating more peace.

Things in Alfred's life were moving along fine when, one morning in 1888, he opened the newspaper and saw his own obituary. As it turned out, Alfred's brother had died, but the local press had accidentally created and run an obituary for Alfred instead. That mistake changed Alfred's legacy. When he saw that the writer of the obituary had summed up his life and his work by giving him the moniker "Merchant of Death," Alfred came face-to-face with the reality of how his days on earth had been spent.

Upset that he could be remembered so negatively, he decided to refocus his remaining time on his original goal—doing something that would help the world around him. With that decision, Alfred drafted a will directing over 90 percent of his net worth to the establishment of Nobel prizes—prizes to be given to, in his words, "those who, during the preceding year, shall have conferred the greatest benefit on mankind."[1] Shortly after his actual death, the first Nobel Prizes were awarded.

How will people remember you? Are you having the kind of impact on the world that you want to have? Have you found the purpose and meaning that your heart longs for? Are you achieving true greatness, or are you, like so

many others, attaining small successes while simultane-
ously realizing that they lack real significance? Consider
the words of author Stephen Covey:

> People often find themselves achieving victories that
> are empty, successes that have come at the expense
> of things they suddenly realize were far more valu-
> able to them. People from every walk of life . . . often
> struggle to achieve a higher income, more recognition
> or a certain degree of professional competence, only
> to find that their drive to achieve their goal blinded
> them to the things that really mattered most and are
> now gone. How different our lives are when we really
> know what is deeply important to us, and, keeping that
> picture in mind, we manage ourselves each day to do
> what really matters most.[2]

Covey contends, as do I, that the way to manage our
lives so that we are focused on what really matters most
is to embrace the idea of principle-centered living. In-
ternalizing and living by correct guiding principles is
the only thing that produces long-term happiness and
success.

The people in our lives and in our world who find
purpose and achieve meaningful goals are those who
live by a strong life-directing principle. Just think back
over some of the greatest, most respected individuals of

our time and you will see that they all lived by a guiding principle. Here are just a few to consider—most you will recognize, though one you may not:

- **Henry David Thoreau** developed and lived by the principle of civil disobedience. His principled living had a hand in the end of slavery and influenced many after him to live by a similar guiding principle.

- **Dr. Martin Luther King Jr.** embraced the principle of nonviolence, originally inspired by Thoreau. Thanks to a life guided by that principle, King spearheaded and effectively led the civil rights movement in the United States.

- **Mother Teresa** lived by the principle of compassion. She devoted nearly half a century to working with the poor, sick, and dying in Calcutta, India. Even now, she remains an icon of compassion.

- **Winston Churchill** understood, lived by, and succeeded through the principle of persistence. In a 1941 speech at the Harrow School, he famously advised the students, "Never give in—never, never, never, never, in nothing great or small, large or petty, never give in except to convictions of honor and good sense."[3]

- **Vince Lombardi** oriented his life around the principle of winning. To him, winning wasn't everything; it was the only thing. And his widespread recognition as one of history's best coaches indicates that he was good at it.

- **Chris Sluder** has oriented his life around the principle of mercy. Although busy with his own work and family concerns, Chris stepped out on faith over a decade ago and created relationships with several orphanages in a destitute area of Kazakhstan. Since then he has worked selflessly to connect dozens of Kazakh orphans with adoptive families through his home church in North Carolina. You may not recognize his name, but because of his guiding principle of mercy, Chris has brought hope and positive change to countless children who otherwise would have very little of either.

Here's the thing about guiding principles: whether we realize it or not, we are all living by one. We either make

---

The content and strength of your dominant guiding principle will directly correlate with the greatness of your life.

---

an intentional choice to center our life on a principle, or we end up living one by default. If we don't determine and embrace a correct principle for ourselves, we will fall into the principle pattern set for us by our closest friends and family—which could easily lead to skewed priorities and unfulfilling years.

The content and strength of your dominant guiding principle will directly correlate with the greatness of your life. With that in mind, take a moment to examine your own heart. What is your current guiding principle? Can you even recognize it? Is it leading you toward success and significance? Is it leading you toward true greatness?

Defining Greatness

You and I receive a lot of mixed messages about what defines a great life. Some people tell us that financial success is the ultimate goal. Others say that fame, and the sense of immortality that comes with it, is true greatness. Still others would say that power is the pinnacle.

In your day-to-day world, you may have your own qualifiers that mark the path toward greatness. You may think that if you do your job well and raise a happy family, then you are achieving greatness. Perhaps you think

> Lives of great men all remind us
> We can make our lives sublime.
> And, departing, leave behind us
> Footprints on the sands of time.
> Henry Wadsworth Longfellow,
> "A Psalm of Life"

that to be great, you need to keep yourself in top physical shape, master a hobby, or always be the life of the party. By the world's standards, greatness can be elusive territory, meaning different things to different people. Ultimately, deep down, we all know that we are searching for the kind of greatness that is inherent in purpose, meaning, and significance, but most of us spend our days treading up a marshy path, not sure if it will ever actually get us to that summit.

In Scripture, on the other hand, we see that God's definition of greatness isn't mysterious or murky at all. When the disciples were having their little spat about which one of them was the greatest, they were looking at greatness through the world's lens (Mark 9:33–37). Jesus wasted no time in letting them know that they were chasing after the wrong goal. What he taught them that day, and on many other occasions, was a principle—a principle worth building our lives on.

The Greatness Principle

While Thoreau, Mother Teresa, and the like understood principled living, the concept didn't start with them. Long before them, Jesus lived his life by the ultimate guiding principle—a principle that has the potential to make us great not only in the world's eyes but also, and more important, in God's eyes. I like to call Jesus's guiding principle "The Greatness Principle."

Scripture never uses the phrase "The Greatness Principle," but Jesus taught on the substance of this principle at least a dozen times. It's also mentioned in Proverbs and discussed by the apostle Paul in Acts and Philippians. Before I give you the actual principle, let's take a look at some of its substantiating teaching, starting with that infamous debate among the disciples:

> After they arrived at Capernaum and settled in a house, Jesus asked his disciples, "What were you discussing out on the road?" But they didn't answer, because they had been arguing about which of them was the greatest. He sat down, called the twelve disciples over to him, and said, "Whoever wants to be first must take last place and be the servant of everyone else." (Mark 9:33–35)

Jesus refers to the principle again in Matthew's account of his conversation with some hypocritical religious leaders: "The greatest among you must be a servant" (Matt. 23:11). In Matthew 20:28, Jesus uses himself as an example to prove his point: "For even the Son of Man came not to be served but to serve others and to give his life as a ransom for many." Are you catching on to the theme?

Before Jesus's ministry even began, King Solomon, the wisest man who ever lived, shined a spotlight on the truth of The Greatness Principle with "The generous will prosper; those who refresh others will themselves be refreshed" (Prov. 11:25). In other words, God will refresh those who bless (read: serve) others.

Later, after Jesus's death and resurrection, Paul underscored the substance of The Greatness Principle in his letter to the Philippian church when he wrote, "Don't look out only for your own interests, but take an interest in others, too. You must have the same attitude that Christ Jesus had" (Phil. 2:4–5). What kind of attitude did Jesus have? He had the attitude of a servant, as we see proven through his own ministry and teaching. Jesus served others in love. Paul goes on to write:

> Though he was God, he did not think of equality with God as something to cling to. Instead, he gave up his divine privileges; he took the humble position of a slave and was born as a human being. (Phil. 2:6–7)

Even though he was the very essence of God, Jesus continually humbled himself and lifted others up. As a result, God blessed him abundantly.

The Greatness Principle is a dominant principle throughout the New Testament. It was the guiding principle in Jesus's life, and it's the primary qualifier of greatness in God's eyes. Those facts alone are reason enough for you and me to make it the standard on which we base our lives. Okay, I've made you wait long enough. Are you ready for the actual principle? Here it is:

> The Greatness Principle: When you bless others, God blesses you.

God wants to bless you. He wants you to live the best life possible. He wants you to understand and achieve true greatness. He sent his Son into this world so that

---

The Greatness Principle: When you bless others, God blesses you.

---

you and I could be reconciled to him and enjoy a full, rich life. As Jesus himself said, "I came that they may have life and have it abundantly" (John 10:10 NASB). But in order to take part in the abundant life Jesus offers, we have to accept his love and embrace his principle of greatness.

A Great Life

To miss The Greatness Principle would mean to miss out on so much of what God has in store for you. It would mean living a life that is less than God's best—a life filled with struggle, a life where you feel distant from God and stagnant in your growth. I know that's not the kind of life you want.

You probably won't get to see it like Alfred Nobel did, but one day your obituary will run in the local newspaper. What will it say? Will it say that you lived a truly great life? That you made the most of the opportunities you were given on this earth and created a legacy that will last? Or will it say that you just got by, doing the best you could? You don't have to settle for mediocrity and nagging discontent. You can be great. You can be abundantly blessed by God. Significance is right in front of you. Do you want it? The decision is yours.

Are you currently living by a guiding principle? If so, what is that principle?

_____

_____

_____

Think about the end of your life: What do you want your friends and family to be able to say about you at your funeral? How do you want your obituary to read? Consider writing out some qualities and accomplishments you'd like to be remembered for.

_____

_____

_____

2

recognizing
great opportunities

Life's most persistent and urgent question is, "What
are you doing for others?"

Martin Luther King Jr.

My son's favorite ride at Disneyworld is Dumbo
the Flying Elephant. In a few years, it will probably be Space Mountain, but right now, he is a big fan of
soaring through the air on Dumbo's back. Those of you
who are parents know what that means—I have ridden
the Dumbo the Flying Elephant ride more times than I
can count. I like to make my son happy, so as long as he

loves Dumbo, so do I. But secretly, I am longing for the Space Mountain days. Everything in due time.

On a recent trip to Disneyworld, we had already had the Dumbo experience three or four times, but my son begged to ride one more time before we left for the day. I obliged and we stepped into the long line to wait our turn. As we shuffled along, a conversation between the couple behind us piqued my interest. They were talking about the Hidden Mickeys they had spotted around the theme park that day. I had never heard of Hidden Mickeys, and we still had a long wait ahead of us, so I struck up a conversation and asked them what they were referring to.

Apparently, as they explained it to me, the early Disney Imagineers (the people who designed the Disney theme parks) hid discreet Mickey Mouse images throughout all of the parks and various attractions. The images are simple—three connected, intersecting circles that look like the outline of Mickey's head and ears—and they are everywhere. They are etched into pavement, painted on the walls of rides, built into the fences, and arranged in the landscaping. Disneyworld is jam-packed with these subtle Hidden Mickeys, but most people don't see them because they don't know to look for them. I sure didn't.

Simple awareness is a powerful thing. When my son and I said our final good-bye to Dumbo and headed toward the parking lot tram, we started seeing Hidden Mickeys everywhere. They began popping out of the woodwork, literally. We had been at the park all day without seeing a single Hidden Mickey, but as soon as we became aware of their existence, we realized we had been surrounded by them all along.

Awakening Awareness

The Greatness Principle and those Hidden Mickeys have something in common. Just as my son and I had to be aware of the Hidden Mickeys before we could see them, you have to become aware of the opportunities to bless others that surround you every day or those opportunities will pass you by sight unseen.

As The Greatness Principle says, when you bless others, God blesses you. It makes sense then that the first step in living by The Greatness Principle is to look for opportunities to bless others every day. You come in contact with countless needs and chances to bless others, but you won't be able to see them until you become aware that they exist.

I'll cut you a little slack here. Your lack of awareness isn't necessarily your fault. By nature, we are selfish people. We tend to walk through life focused on our own interests—what we want, what we need, what we have to do to get ahead, what makes us feel good—rather than focused on the people around us. It's all too easy

---

Look for opportunities to bless others every day.

---

for us to fall into the "every man for himself" attitude by default, forgetting time and again that life is bigger than our personal concerns.

We aren't the first generation to struggle with self-ishness either. This element of human nature has been rearing its head throughout history. When Paul wrote his famed letter to the Philippian church in the early 60s AD, he already felt the need to remind his readers to live outwardly focused lives. I mentioned these verses in the last chapter, but they are worth examining again:

> Don't be selfish; don't try to impress others. Be humble, thinking of others as better than yourselves. Don't look out only for your own interests, but take an interest in others, too. (Phil. 2:3–4)

Paul's words ring as true—arguably even truer—today as they did when they were written so many centuries ago.

Interestingly, even though we are self-focused by nature, most of us know that focusing on ourselves doesn't bring much satisfaction or joy. If we're honest, we can admit that we feel most alive and happiest when we shift our focus off of ourselves and onto other people. It's no wonder a book that opens with the line "It's not about you" became, next to the Bible, one of the most bestselling books in the history of the world.[1]

We all know that it's not about us, and deep down in the recesses of our soul we are hungry to connect with purposes bigger than our own. We want more for ourselves. We want to bless other people; we want to receive God's blessing. Still, we fall into the rut of making it about us. Here's some good news: you and I can break out of that rut by learning to become aware.

God puts people in your path every day that you can bless—people he wants you to bless. But if you aren't walking in awareness, you are missing those opportunities. If you want to live by The Greatness Principle—if you want to experience the abundant life God has for you, find significance, and grow in spiritual maturity—you have to be aware of the needs around you and be on the lookout for opportunities to bless other people.

Take a moment to think back over the last few months of your life. Have you missed opportunities to serve other people? Have you glossed over a co-worker's need to confide in you? Have you ignored openings to make your spouse's life a little easier? Have you taken every opportunity you should have to encourage your children?

Maybe at the time, you didn't even realize that you were missing out on blessing others, but now, looking back, you see chances that have slipped through your fingers.

If you want to be great and receive God's incredible blessing, you have to consciously engage in your everyday world. Practice becoming aware of the opportunities right in front of you to make someone's life a little better, to help someone in need, to give an encouraging word, or to lighten a load. Once you open your eyes to what's around you, you will see Hidden Mickeys—I mean, opportunities to bless others—everywhere.

The Great Compassion

Jesus often taught on the importance of seeing and seizing opportunities to bless others. In Matthew 25:34–40, a passage that has become commonly known as "The Great Compassion," Jesus says:

> Then the King will say to those on the right . . . "For I was hungry, and you fed me. I was thirsty, and you gave me a drink. I was a stranger, and you invited me into your home. I was naked, and you gave me clothing. I was sick, and you cared for me. I was in prison, and you visited me." Then these righteous ones will reply, "Lord, when did we ever see you hungry and feed you? Or thirsty and give you something to

drink? Or a stranger and show you hospitality? Or naked and give you clothing? When did we ever see you sick or in prison, and visit you?" And the King will say, "I tell you the truth, when you did it to one of the least of these my brothers and sisters, you were doing it to me!"

In this passage, Jesus points out six specific opportunities to bless others. Keep in mind the list is not exhaustive, by any means. You could think of these opportunities as the first six of a thousand Hidden Mickeys.

Don't assume that Jesus's references here are merely superficial. That wouldn't be like Jesus at all. Every situation he mentions presents us with a literal opportunity and a more figurative opportunity to engage with the people God puts around us. Let's take a closer look at each of the six scenarios Jesus describes.

1. I was hungry and you fed me. Since you and I have full stomachs most of the time, we easily forget that there are hungry men, women, and children all around us. In your city or town, and in cities and towns throughout America, scores of people will go to bed tonight with empty stomachs. According to the organization "Feeding America," one in every six Americans doesn't have enough to eat, including more than one in five children.[2] Around the world, the numbers are much more staggering.

Those of us who have been blessed with plenty have a moral obligation, responsibility, and clear call from Scripture to help those who are less fortunate. But our lack of awareness keeps us at a distance. We blindly eat our three squares—in a lot of cases, we well overeat those three squares—without so much as a thought for the family down the road struggling to put food on the table. When we open our eyes to the problem of hunger, however, our perspective begins to shift and we begin to see chances to help all around us. For specific opportunities to serve the hungry, check first with your local church. They may have a food pantry you can help stock, regular outreach opportunities at a local homeless shelter, or other similar ministry initiatives you can get involved in.

Hunger exists in more than one form. While the people closest to you may have enough to eat, many of them are desperately trying to soothe the ache of emotional and spiritual hunger. They are hungry for acceptance and approval, for friendship and love. You and I have opportunities to feed emotionally hungry people every day, but we have to walk in a state of awareness, or those opportunities will pass us by. We can feed the hungry people in our lives with a kind word, with a touch, by reminding them of their worth and telling them that we love them. Most important, we can point them toward the love of God, so they can find their true fulfillment in him.

2. I was thirsty and you gave me a drink. Living in the United States, we have clean water flowing out of every spigot in our homes and bottled water readily available at every market and convenience store. We are privileged. Around the world it's a different story. More than a billion people live without access to clean water. Did you know that two million people die every year as a result of water-related illness?[3] Most of us walk around, full water bottle in hand, completely unaware. But as we open our eyes to the reality of the thirsty people in our world, we begin to see that we have the opportunity to help.

Your church may provide clean water to thirsty people in ways you don't even realize. At my church, The Journey, we support many missionaries around the world. As part of ministering to the communities they are called to, these missionaries often work to meet the basic need for clean water by digging wells and building systems that can provide it. Check to see if your church partners with similar missionaries or organizations. If they don't, there are many American organizations that focus on making clean water available across the globe.

Again, outside of the literal interpretation of this call, there is a heavy spiritual implication as well. Our lives are filled with spiritually thirsty people—people who are thirsty for love, encouragement, and forgiveness. Open your eyes to the thirsty people all around you and you'll begin to see their need. You possess the ability to quench their thirst in small ways every day.

3. I was a stranger and you invited me into your home. I have a friend in North Carolina who pastors a large, thriving church. Chris Sluder, the mercy-minded gentleman I mentioned in chapter 1, is a member there. A real estate agent by trade, Chris took the initiative to step outside of his comfort zone during the height of his career and create a connection with some orphanages in a remote area of Kazakhstan. After visiting Kazakhstan and seeing the conditions the orphans were living in, he arranged for about a dozen of the kids to travel to North Carolina and stay with various host families. The families opened their homes to these children and did their best to provide them with a good experience and show them a reflection of God's love. As a result of the arrangement, many of the Kazakh kids ended up being adopted.

My friend and his family didn't host a child, but they did end up falling in love with one—a ten-year-old girl who was staying with another family. They felt an undeniable pull to bring this little girl—this stranger, this orphan—into their home for good, so they began the arduous process of adopting her. Now twenty, she has been fully grafted into my friend's family. While she was still unknown, they opened their home and their lives to her, and today she is a happy, vibrant, loving member of the family.

Our relationship with God isn't all that different. Before you and I knew him, we were strangers to his love. But God opened his home to us and invited us in. With that example as your guide, be aware of the opportunities around you to show love to strangers—to invite them into your life and community, to befriend them and give them support when they need it. You have this opportunity when someone visits your church, when you see an opening to make a new friend, when you come across someone you have the power to help by inviting him or her into your home. Be wise as you approach this command, but always be on the lookout to be a blessing to strangers.

4. I was naked and you gave me clothing. Our over-stuffed closets are a visual reminder of the opportunity we have to help people who aren't as fortunate as we are. While they may not be walking around naked, there are people all around us who are in desperate need of clothes, warm coats, and shoes. Your church may sponsor periodic clothing drives or have ongoing partnerships in place to help clothe the needy. Check with your pastor or small group leader to see how you can get involved. Many great organizations also exist to help provide people with clothing and other basic necessities. The Salvation Army is a prime example. Choose to be aware of this need so that you will be able to bless others when the opportunity arises.

5. I was sick and you cared for me. Life is so hectic that we often gloss over the sicknesses of others. We tell them we hope they feel better as we say a little prayer of thanksgiving for our own health. The truth is that sickness is a major vulnerability and, if we make ourselves aware, provides us with a great opportunity to serve others. Whether we simply take soup to a friend with a cold or sit with a family member who is facing a terminal illness, the opportunities to be a blessing are everywhere.

Physically speaking, we all get sick from time to time, but many people also live with continual spiritual and emotional sickness. Plenty of people that you come into contact with every day are facing crises of self-esteem, loneliness, and questions of worth. A simple encouraging word or other expression of love can go a long way toward helping the spiritually and emotionally sick feel better.

6. I was in prison and you visited me. People who find themselves on the fringes of our society, whatever the circumstances, are the ones who need the most love and forgiveness. Working with inmates is a more specialized call than the five calls mentioned above, but it is an important way to serve others and a powerful tool for reaching the hearts of those who have made choices that have landed them outside of accepted society. Let this verse serve as a reminder that we are to be aware of those who are outcast and that we are to show them care and concern.

Of course, we can't leave this discussion without shifting awareness to people who are living in prisons of their own making. People in your life and mine are living in prisons of shame, prisons of despair, prisons of hurt, prisons of want, and many other prisons of their own design. Again, we need to open our eyes to the pain of the people in our sphere of influence. Then and only then will we be in a position where we can even begin to embrace The Greatness Principle and bless them.

For more ways to help, check with your local church and visit www.TheGreatnessPrinciple.com.

> There is a loftier ambition than merely to stand high in the world. It is to stoop down and lift mankind a little higher.
>
> Henry Van Dyke

Descending to Greatness

Early on in my Christian faith, I mistakenly bought into the myth of ascending greatness. I used to think God would put his plans, purposes, and blessings for me on the lowest shelf, in the same way grocers put kids' cereals on the bottom supermarket shelves. I assumed that as I matured, he would begin placing his will for me higher and higher and that, as I reached for it, I would be continually ascending to greatness.

Actually, just the opposite is true. As Christ followers, you and I don't ascend to greatness. Rather, we descend to greatness as we become aware of the needs around us and put those needs before our own. In other words, with every step that you take in your Christian life, God moves the target lower and lower. He wants to know if you will be willing to serve as he served. He wants to know if you will humble yourself as he did. He wants to know if you will bow before him and acknowledge that you can't achieve greatness on your own, but only through his power and principles.

God gives us open doors to humble ourselves and bless others every single day. Now that you are aware of a few of the opportunities already around you, I challenge you to be on the lookout for more. Look for chances to bless others in big ways and small ways. As you move forward in a spirit of awareness, God is going to bring opportunities out of the woodwork, guide you toward the ones he wants you to act on, and then bless you greatly in return.

What steps could you take to be more aware of the needs and opportunities surrounding you?

_____

_____

_____

List some concrete ways you could bless those around you in the coming weeks.

_____

_____

_____

3

seizing significance

I am only one; but still I am one. I cannot do everything, but still I can do something. I will not refuse to do the something I can do.

Helen Keller

I'm not much of a skier, but one of my good friends is practically a pro. He's also a bit of an adrenaline junky—but that's beside the point. A few weeks ago we got together for dinner and he was telling me about one of his most recent ski adventures. He had traveled to Antarctica and spent a week and a half skiing many rugged, never-before-skied peaks. At his wife's insistence, he skied with a professional guide who knew which passes he should tackle and which ones he should avoid. Describing the beauty of the area and the rush of skiing such uncharted territory, my friend said to me, "Nelson, that was one of the most incredible adventures of my life."

As my friend talked about following his guide across snowy peaks and being totally dependent on his expert discretion in terms of where to point downhill and where not to, I couldn't help but make the connection between his experience skiing and our experience with God. We may not be dropping out of a helicopter in the middle of Antarctica (yes, he did that), but you and I are definitely on an adventure with God. We face new, uncertain terrain every day, and the only way to make sure we stay on the right path is to look to God as our guide. Just as my friend was dependent on his guide's know-how to make it to the bottom of each mountain safely, we are dependent on God's wisdom and expertise to guide us down the paths he has in store for us and to steer us away from the ones he doesn't.

The Great Adventure

Wars. Floods. Earthquakes. Divorce. Death. Loneliness. Financial crises. Broken relationships. Sickness. Poverty. These things aren't quite as endearing as the Hidden Mickeys we discussed in the last chapter, but when you open your eyes to the opportunities around you to bless others, these are the types of need creators you will start seeing everywhere.

Your new sense of awareness may quickly become overwhelming. Your heart will break for the people you want to help, and you will have to come to terms with the reality that you can't serve everyone. You can't meet every need. After all, you are just one person. Moreover, God doesn't expect you to meet every opportunity that comes your way. Not every potential chance to bless someone is an open door to do so.

You may be thinking, "Wait a minute. Didn't you just say not to be selfish and to be on the lookout for ways to bless others?" I did. You do need to turn from selfishness and be watching for ways to bless others every day. But as you do, keep in mind that God doesn't expect you to be able to bless every person you see. That would be completely unrealistic. The needs of the world at large, and the needs of your own personal circle, are way too huge and complex for you to meet on your own.

That said, don't let the overwhelming number of opportunities to serve keep you from taking advantage of the right opportunities to serve. As I mentioned, you are on an adventure with God, and his guidance is vital. Think of the needs and opportunities that surround you every day as the rugged, uncharted paths of a massive mountain. God is right alongside you directing you to move toward one path rather than another, showing you which trails you should ski and which ones you should leave for someone else.

The truth is, my friend couldn't possibly have skied every potential run he saw. He would have burned out too quickly and ultimately risked his own safety. Simi-

---

Initiate action as God guides you.

---

larly, we can't walk through every open door we come across; we can't seize every opportunity we see to serve. Thankfully, as we start becoming aware of the needs and opportunities around us, we can heed the instruction of our knowledgeable guide, who will tell us where to direct our energy.

The second step of living by The Greatness Principle, then, is not to try to serve everyone in every way, but rather to initiate action as God guides you. Initiating action as God guides you is the key element of moving from having an awareness of the opportunities around you to becoming obedient in meeting the needs God wants you to meet. When you see a need, pause and ask God if it's something he wants you to be involved in, and then be open to his answer. We can trust God to guide our lives and our efforts in the best direction possible. In Psalm 32:8 he promises, "I will guide you along the best pathway for your life. I will advise you and watch over you." Instead of barreling ahead on our own, we simply have to trust in his wisdom.

Go. No. Slow.

I imagine that when my friend was on the mountain with his guide, they developed some signals to communicate with each other throughout the journey. For example, if my friend saw a path he wanted to ski down, I'm sure he had a way to get his guide's attention and point it out. Then the guide probably gave him one of three signals: (1) okay, (2) not a chance, or (3) proceed with caution. When an opportunity to get involved in being a blessing presents itself, God generally directs us in one of three similar ways. He will either say go, no, or slow.

When God says *go*, that's a clear invitation to go ahead and get involved in the opportunity in front of you. Sometimes, however, he'll say *no* to let you know that even though you see a need, it's not one he intends for you to meet. If God doesn't want you to seize an opportunity you see, you can be sure of two things. First of all, he has something else that he wants you to do, and the current opportunity would only be a distraction from

"Stand still"—keep the posture of an upright man, ready for action, expecting further orders, cheerfully and patiently awaiting the directing voice; and it will not be long ere God shall say to you, as distinctly as Moses said it to the people of Israel, "Go forward."

Charles Spurgeon

the better opportunity. Second, he has someone else in mind to meet the need in question. The other answer God may give you is *slow*. In other words, he may want you to get involved in a certain opportunity, but just not yet. You need to wait until the timing is right.

To be in tune with how God is directing you, ask for his guidance and stay sensitive to his voice through quality time in prayer and reading his Word. Then you will be able to sift through the many opportunities to bless that you see each day and put your effort and energy into blessing the exact people God wants you to bless in the exact way and at the exact time he wants you to bless them.

Go. No. Slow.

Go—Get involved.
No—Not for you.
Slow—Not now, but maybe later.

Doing What Comes Naturally

While keeping the idea of go, no, slow in mind, let's examine a couple of other realities concerning where and how you should serve others. First, never use waiting on God as an excuse to keep you from blessing people in small, obvious ways. God's go, no, and slow responses pertain more to large, overarching needs and long-term involvements than to small, direct chances to help the people in your life. There's no need to pray about those small opportunities; he has already told us how to respond to them:

> Do not withhold good from those who deserve it when it's in your power to help them. If you can help your neighbor now, don't say, "Come back tomorrow, and then I'll help you." (Prov. 3:27–28)

Don't check your God-given common sense at the door. If you see someone drop his wallet, you don't need to have a conversation with God before you decide to pick it up and give it back to him. If your church or a community organization is having a canned food drive, you don't necessarily need to pray about grabbing some cans of food and donating them. If your great aunt lives in a nursing home, it's not imperative to seek God's direction over whether or not to go spend an afternoon with her. If your co-worker is upset, you don't need guidance on whether or not to offer a word of encouragement.

These are easy, obvious opportunities that God puts in your path for you to bless other people. Of course, when it comes to bigger chances to serve—something like stepping into a regular or high-level volunteer position in your church, committing to ongoing volunteer work at a shelter, or donating a large amount of money to a family in need—make sure you are being sensitive to God's guidance.

Second, as you seek God's guidance in bigger opportunities and decisions, pay close attention to how he has naturally wired you. God created you the way you are for a reason. In his letter to the Roman church Paul writes, "In his grace, God has given us different gifts for doing certain things well" (Rom. 12:6). Paul's assertion is echoed many times over throughout the Scriptures. God has molded us and made each of us for a particular purpose (Ps. 139:13–16). A manifestation of the Holy Spirit is given to each and every one of us so that we can use it to do our part (1 Cor. 12:7). We have been uniquely crafted and formed into the individuals we are by a God who loves us. And guess what? He allows us to know ourselves pretty well.

I can guarantee that you already have a natural passion for serving in a way that relates to the innate gifts God has given you and the current circumstances where he has placed you. Too often we get caught up in feeling like we need to take this spiritual gifts assessment or that personality test before we can know where we should serve; or we think that the assessment we took twenty years ago is still the best indicator of our makeup. In my experience, while such tests have their place, they can also be major roadblocks. Nine times out of ten, even the most advanced tests simply provide confirmation that you should be seizing the opportunities you feel drawn toward in your heart. Not to mention, your passion and place of service may change over time, as your life situation changes.

Stay open and sensitive to God's guidance, act on small opportunities that present themselves to you daily, and pay attention to your passions and gifts. When you do those three things, you will be able to step forward into the world ready to bless others enormously.

Five Ways to Bless Others

When you know that God is guiding you toward a specific opportunity to serve, take a moment to ask yourself, "How can I best respond in this situation?" The right answer will generally be found in one of the five primary ways you and I can bless others:

Give Your Time: Sometimes all it takes to bless another person is a little bit of your time. At The Journey, we have hundreds of volunteers who show up for church an hour early every week to make sure that the services run smoothly. By giving a small piece of their time to serve others through ushering, handing out programs, or simply greeting people with a smile, these volunteers are a big blessing to everyone who attends our services.

Share Your Talent: As we have discussed, you are gifted in specific ways. Your gifts have been given to you in order to build up God's kingdom, so don't waste them by sitting on the sidelines. Be ready to put them into action. If you are a gifted singer or musician, you may be called to meet a need on your church's worship team. If you are good at relating to children, perhaps you can use your gifting to help a single mom in your neighborhood with child care. Be on the lookout for ways to use your specific talents and gifts to bless others.

Invest Your Treasure: While all of us as Christ followers are called to invest financially in God's work, sometimes you will see a need or an opportunity to go above and beyond with your giving. Be sensitive to God's guiding in this area. Allow him to open your hand and use you as a conduit to bless others financially. (For an in-depth look at the power of honoring God with your finances, see my book *The Generosity Ladder: Your Next Step to Financial Peace* [Baker Books, 2010].)

Encourage with Your Talk: Sometimes an encouraging word may be all you have to offer someone in need. Don't underestimate the power of this blessing. The right words spoken at the right time can bring peace and comfort in many difficult situations.

Proclaim Your Testimony: No matter how you are directed to meet the needs and opportunities around you, always be quick to turn the conversation toward God. Sometimes you will be able to share a few words about your faith alongside another way of blessing someone, and other times this will be all you can do. Still, telling someone you will pray for them, and then doing it, is one of the best ways to be a blessing. Inviting them to church to hear a message that relates to what they are going through is another. Just make sure you are connecting your desire to help them with the love and example of the God you serve. We'll discuss this in much more detail in the next chapter. (For a free, downloadable guide on how to write your testimony, visit www.TheGreatnessPrinciple.com.)

Initiating action as God guides you—that is, being open to his direction as he leads you along the best paths—hinges on your willingness to move from an awareness of the needs and opportunities around you to obedience in meeting them. Since obedience is the key, it's not surprising that God also made it a catalyst to our loving him and loving others even more. Consider this passage from C. S. Lewis's classic text *Mere Christianity*:

> I may repeat, "Do as you would be done by" till I am blue in the face, but I cannot really carry it out till I love my neighbor as myself, and I cannot learn to love my neighbor as myself till I learn to love God; and I cannot learn to love God except by learning to obey Him.[1]

By learning to obey him, we find ourselves willing and able to bless others from a place of authentic concern and love (something we'll talk more about in chapter 6). When we embrace this truth and begin to act on it, we will be living out the first half of The Greatness Principle and positioning ourselves to be humble recipients of the second half.

What are some examples of easy, obvious ways you can bless others?

_____

_____

_____

What are some examples of larger opportunities to which God may be calling you?

_____

_____

_____

What are some activities you naturally gravitate toward that could be indicative of ways you could serve?

_____

_____

_____

4

credit where credit is due

> Good people doing good works in the world is not enough to fully accomplish what God wants done. God seeks to reveal Himself in majesty and truth in our generation—and to do so through us.
>
> Bruce Wilkinson

My wife and I go on a date once a month. Between my hectic schedule and all of Kelley's responsibilities, it can be hard to pin a night down, but twosome time is a priority so we do whatever needs to be done to get date nights on the calendar. Sometimes we keep our dates low-key (think pizza and a movie, maybe even on the couch at home), but sometimes we take things up a notch and go to a new play or a trendy restaurant. Whatever we have planned, I am a stickler about ensuring that the details are in order and that everything is set up to go exactly like we want.

For one of our recent date nights, I made a reservation at a restaurant in town that was, apparently, the hot new place. A few of our friends had been there and raved about it. Thanks to all the hype, I had to make reservations three weeks in advance to get a table. When the night came, Kelley and I got dressed up, dropped our son off at a friend's house, and headed downtown. I was impressed as soon as we pulled up to the restaurant. The building was gorgeous. The ambiance inside was warm and inviting. The aromas swirling around were unbelievable. As the hostess led us past a jazz quartet to our table, I just knew that this would be a great night—a perfect night. That is, until our waiter approached the table.

As soon as Henry (I know his name thanks only to his name tag) walked up, the mood began to crumble. With no greeting and no eye contact, he pulled out his notepad and grunted, "Do you know what you want?" A little taken aback, I said, "Um, no, we actually just sat down. I think we need . . ." Before I could finish my sentence, Henry shoved his notepad back into his pocket and walked away.

Now, I can dismiss such behavior at a dive or a diner, but this place was neither of those things. Not by a long shot. This restaurant was meant to be an experience—the kind of place where you spend time with the menu, ask questions of the waiter, and make sure you choose the perfect dish. It's the kind of place where you linger over your appetizer before the meal comes and linger over your meal before dessert. You get the picture. To say that Henry's attitude did not match the atmosphere is an understatement. He was our server for the evening, but I knew immediately he had zero interest in serving us.

Still, all things work together for good. Even though Henry's service didn't get any better throughout the meal, his attitude led Kelley and me to an interesting conversation. We found ourselves talking about the idea of living and serving in a way that makes the gospel of Jesus appealing to those who don't believe in him. In to-day's world, where faith is a buzzword and moral relativism reigns, how do we let people know that our inherent joy and the good things we do are a reflection of God's love and excellence, and not just a result of us being nice people? (I love these kinds of discussions with my wife.)

This particular date night happened to be around the time that I was beginning to uncover and understand the power of The Greatness Principle. In my study I had been digging into the truth that, as Christ followers—

and therefore as his representatives in the world—our call is to live with his attitude and then to intentionally reflect any credit or praise that comes our way back to God. With that in mind, Kelley and I made a decision to serve Henry in a very practical way. Even though logic would suggest that he didn't deserve to be blessed with an unusually gracious tip, we decided to give him one anyway—and to take the opportunity to deliberately tie our giving back to God.

At the end of our meal, Henry ran my credit card and brought the receipt back to the table. Instead of including his tip on the receipt, I wanted to give him cash, so that I would have the chance to put it right in his hand. I pulled an amount that would be considered significant even for good service out of my wallet and waited until he came back to the table to pick up the receipt. Now, you may think that since I am a pastor, bringing up God is always an easy thing to do. You would be wrong. I was a little nervous about what I was going to say to Henry.

As I saw him walking back toward us, I had a decision to make. I could either hand him the money with a simple word of thanks and let him think I was a great guy, or I could tell him I was giving him the tip as an outward, tangible sign of God's goodness and love toward him. In other words, I could keep quiet and take the credit for myself, or I could focus the attention toward God.

Well, even though it was slightly intimidating, I handed Henry the money and said, "Thank you, Henry. I want to bless you with this tip as a practical expression of God's love for you. My wife and I appreciate your service tonight." In keeping with character, Henry grunted a thank-you and walked away without looking at the amount in his hand. But that was okay. I had done what I should, and I knew he would be touched by it.

Be a Mirror

Jesus, the greatest example of a servant ever to walk the earth, blessed people in a multitude of ways—bigger and more extravagant ways than we will ever be able to do. He provided for the needy; he healed sick people; he brought dead people back to life; ultimately, he laid down his own life for us on the cross. But throughout his earthly ministry and even in his crucifixion, Jesus made clear that the motive behind every single thing he did was to bring glory to his Father in heaven. He had no interest in winning accolades for himself. In fact, once, when the people around him were questioning his intentions, Jesus said as clearly as possible, "If I want glory for myself, it doesn't count. But it is my Father who will glorify me" (John 8:54).

When you begin living out The Greatness Principle by blessing the people in your world, onlookers will inevitably give you credit for the good you are doing. You'll get pats on the back and words of praise. That's when you will have a choice to make, just like the one I had to make with Henry. You can either focus the attention coming your way back toward God, or you can keep quiet and accept the acclaim.

Before you are tempted to take the path of least resistance and hold on to that credit, pay close attention to what Jesus has to say about the two options right on the heels of telling us how to be great:

> The greatest among you must be a servant. But those who exalt themselves will be humbled, and those who humble themselves will be exalted. (Matt. 23:11–12)

If you let people think that you are the source of the good works you are doing, you are, in essence, exalting yourself. Jesus says that you will be humbled. Believe me, humbling yourself is a much better option than being humbled. Not to mention, when you humble yourself, God will exalt you. Don't you think that God's exaltation will far outweigh the exaltation you would receive from taking the credit yourself? No question.

Don't misunderstand me: I'm not suggesting that you embrace some kind of false humility. When you step out of your comfort zone and bless another person, you will have done something great. It's fine for you to accept thanks. Just be quick to point the attention back to the

---

Focus the attention toward God.

---

greatness of the one you are really serving. It's a good idea to pray a prayer of thanks when we receive praise to acknowledge the one to whom all glory belongs. As the psalmist wrote, "Not to us, O LORD, not to us, but to your name goes all the glory for your unfailing love and faithfulness" (Ps. 115:1). Let your service be a mirror that reflects God's unfailing love and faithfulness, rather than one that reflects your own image. It's all for him anyway.

Proper Perspective

In his letter to the Colossian church, Paul wrote:

> Work willingly at whatever you do, as though you were working for the Lord rather than for people. (Col. 3:23)

How would your attitude toward service be different if you took Paul's admonition to heart? What if you approached every opportunity to serve as if you were actually serving God instead of another person? Would you be more willing to get involved where you know you should? Would you be more likely to steer clear of halfheartedness and focus on serving with excellence? Would you be quicker to take on a spirit of humility?

I was struck by the truth of Paul's words early in my career as a pastor. While attending a conference, I took part in a breakout session where I found myself in a room with some discouraged church leaders. These pastors and high-level volunteers told story after story about how they were becoming frustrated in their efforts to serve others. People kept disappointing them; their motives were misunderstood; their long hours and hard work seemed to be to no avail. After listening to about a dozen of these stories, the gentleman leading the conference asked a simple question: "Who are you serving?"

At first the men and women who had been venting didn't get it. They answered that they were serving their congregations, of course; they were serving the people God had put in their path. The leader told them, "As long as you are working for people, you will end up frustrated, burnt out, and even hurt. But when you stop working for the people in front of you and instead work for God through them, you'll minister more effectively and find more joy in the process."

Thanks to that experience, I remind myself every day that the reason I do what I do is to serve God. The same goes for you. When you start seizing opportunities to bless the people in your world, remember that God is the one you are really working for. That simple adjustment in your perspective will make it much easier to focus any and all attention back toward him.

A Reflection of Excellence

When it comes to bringing God glory, good just isn't good enough. In 1 Corinthians 10:31, Paul steps up the stakes on his statement about working for God rather than people with "whatever you do, do it all for the *glory* of God" (emphasis added). Working for God to the glory of God inherently means that you and I are to be excellent in all that we do. When a door opens for you to give someone an immediate blessing, bless him or her with excellence. When God guides you to serve in a particular area, serve with excellence. Approach every opportunity you have to engage another person with the very best that you have to give.

Consider these thoughts from Willow Creek founder Bill Hybels on our imperative to be excellent:

In response to His holiness and greatness, in gratitude for His monumental sacrifice for us, our attitude ought to be to pay tribute to Him with the best we can offer. I'm not talking about obsessive perfectionism but rather an attitude of excellence that permeates all we do. . . . After all, what we do as Christians reflects on the Christ we serve. Inevitably, there's something about doing a task in a quality fashion that lifts our spirits and makes our souls feel noble. Beyond that, others are inspired. When the bar of performance is raised, everybody is motivated to do their best. And seekers are attracted, because they are accustomed to striving for high standards in the marketplace.[1]

Excellence can be a sliding scale, however, so how do you know when you are achieving it? Let me give you a definition of excellence that I want you to memorize and remind yourself of often: excellence is doing the best you can with what you've been given. It's that simple, yet monumental. Excellence on our part echoes the excellence of our God.

Excellence is doing the best you can with what you've been given.

When you consistently do the best you can with what you've been given—and connect the attention that your excellence brings back to the God you are serving—you will be reflecting his glory to the world. You'll be shining, just as Jesus called you to when he said, "Let your light shine before men in such a way that they may see your good works, and glorify your Father who is in heaven" (Matt. 5:16 NASB).

How would serving "as if unto the Lord" influence how you serve?

_____

_____

_____

Can you name some specific examples of how you could display this outlook in your own life?

_____

_____

_____

5

the power
of positive expectation

> However many blessings we expect from God, His
> infinite liberality will always exceed all our wishes and
> our thoughts.
>
> John Calvin

There is a lot of power in positive expectation when it's based in truth. If fully embraced, it has the potential to transform your world. Biblical positive expectation is not to be confused with the positive-thinking techniques that permeate pop psychology; it goes much deeper. True positive expectation can be realized only as we discover all that God says in his word about how he wants to bless us, and as we choose to actively believe what he says.

So what exactly is positive expectation? It's the state of knowing that you are partnering with God to do his work in the world and believing that he is going to be true to his promise to bless you in return. Many people

---

Positive expectation is the state of knowing that you are partnering with God to do his work in the world and believing that he is going to be true to his promise to bless you in return.

---

want God to rain down blessing on them, but they don't want to surrender their will to him in obedience. They aren't willing to think and act like Jesus, as we've been discussing in these pages. These people will never experience true positive expectation. They are looking for a genie in a bottle rather than an authentic relationship with God.

On the other hand, when you humble yourself before God and commit to serving him selflessly, you can walk in positive expectation of God's blessing and goodness in your life. As you honor God with your service, he will honor you in turn. Jesus made that promise himself:

Anyone who wants to be my disciple must follow me, because my servants must be where I am. And the Father will honor anyone who serves me. (John 12:26)

Consider all of the implications of this verse. First of all, it underscores our imperative to think and act like Jesus. Jesus was a servant. You and I, as disciples, are his servants and therefore God's servants. We are called to be where he is in thought and in action. Jesus goes on to say that God will honor us for serving him. The way God honors people is through his blessing. When we are honoring God through serving him by serving others, he will bless us in return. Or as The Greatness Principle puts it: *When you bless others, God blesses you.*

Expecting God's Blessings

Are you uncomfortable with the idea of expecting God to bless you? If you are, you're not alone. A lot of Christians get nervous at the thought of expecting the God of the universe to pour blessings into their lives. But again, positive expectation is rooted in believing what God says in his Word. If you know and believe what God says about his blessings, then you won't feel strange about expecting them.

The Greatness Principle itself is what is often referred to as an if-then statement. That is, *if* x comes to pass, *then* y will come to pass. *If* you bless others, *then* God will bless

---

Expect God to bless you.

---

you. While if-then terminology is rooted in the world of computer programming, the concept is ancient. The Bible is filled with if-then statements. All the way back in Genesis 18:26, God said, "If I find fifty righteous people in Sodom, I will spare the entire city for their sake." In Isaiah 1:19, he said, "If you will only obey me, you will have plenty to eat." In 1 John 1:9, John wrote, "But if we confess our sins to him, he is faithful and just to forgive us our sins and to cleanse us from all wickedness."

Not only is the Bible full of if-then instruction; it also promises time and time again that when we bless others, God will bless us in return. Let's take a look at just three of those promises:

- **Luke 6:38:** "Give, and you will receive. Your gift will return to you in full—pressed down, shaken together to make room for more, running over, and poured into your lap. The amount you give will determine the amount you get back."

Jesus is talking about financial blessing. He promises that if you bless others financially, you will be financially blessed in return. You simply can't give without receiving. He even expands on the promise by telling us that there is a direct correlation between how much we bless others and how much we will be blessed. (For more on what the Bible has to say about financial peace and blessing, see my book *The Generosity Ladder: Your Next Step to Financial Peace* [Baker Books, 2010].)

- **Matthew 5:7:** "God blesses those who are merciful, for they will be shown mercy."

Biblical mercy can be defined as love in action. If you show mercy to others, you will receive God's blessing. He will show you mercy. There is no ambiguity here; again, this is a biblical promise that if we do *x*, God will bless us in return.

- **Proverbs 11:25:** "The generous will prosper; those who refresh others will themselves be refreshed."

As you may remember from chapter 1, these words written by King Solomon perfectly undergird The Greatness Principle. Reread the verse, substituting the word *bless* for the word *refresh*. Those who bless others will be blessed. That is God's promise to us.

Even though the assurance of God's blessing is real and available, you may still feel a little odd about expecting it. After all, shouldn't you want to bless people purely out of a servant's heart, with no expectation of anything in return? Well, sort of. Yes, you should selflessly obey God when he leads you toward opportunities to serve.

If you're not expecting the blessing, you will either miss it or fail to give God the credit.

You have an *if* to fulfill before the *then* can take place—and that *if* can be executed properly only out of a heart that is in alignment with God's. Your first thought should never be, "What's in it for me," but rather, "How can I help?" Still, expecting God's blessing sweetens the process and puts you in true partnership with God and his plans to use you greatly in this world.

Positive expectation will, by its very nature, cause you to be on the lookout for God's blessing. As we established with those Hidden Mickeys, when you know to look for something you start to see it. So, as you expect blessing, you'll begin recognizing it when it shows up. Then, you'll have the opportunity to thank God for his blessing and turn the attention back toward him. If you're not expecting the blessing, you will either miss it or fail to give God the credit. None of us want to be caught blindly taking in God's blessing without proper thanksgiving, so we would be wise to continually walk in positive expectation.

Recognizing God's Blessing

You may have heard the old story about the college senior—let's call him Justin—who had his eye on a bright red Corvette at a dealership close to his parents' house. In the weeks leading up to his graduation, Justin dropped subtle and not-so-subtle hints to his dad that he wanted the Corvette as his graduation present. After all, his parents were wealthy and there was no reason they couldn't buy it for him.

The morning of graduation, Justin woke up thinking about the Corvette. He could hardly concentrate on the commencement ceremony; his mind was already flying down the highway in his new car. After the diplomas had been passed out, Justin's parents hosted a blowout graduation party for him at their house. Finally, the moment came when Justin's dad tapped him on the shoulder and asked him to join him in the den. Justin knew this was it; he was about to get exactly what he wanted.

Once they were seated in the den, Justin's dad handed him a package. He unwrapped it to find a beautifully bound Bible inscribed with his name. Disappointed and angry, Justin pointed a finger at his father and said, "With all your money you give me a Bible? You knew I wanted that car, Dad!" Then he stormed out of the house, leaving the book behind.

Years later, when Justin had become a successful businessman himself, he got a call that his dad was sick. Justin's explosion on graduation day had caused a rift in the relationship, and he hadn't seen his father since. When he got the phone call, though, he decided he should go home and mend things. Unfortunately, before Justin could get there, he received another call saying that his dad had passed away and that everything had been willed to him.

When Justin finally got to his parents' house to take care of what needed taking care of, he was full of sadness and regret. As he was going through some books and papers in the den, he found the still-new Bible from his graduation day. He couldn't hold back the tears as he opened the Bible and started turning the pages. Suddenly, a car key dropped from an envelope that had been taped to the Bible's back cover. It was on a key ring from the neighborhood dealership. On the back of the key ring, Justin's father had written, "Congratulations, Son! Celebrate with a new Corvette!"

You and I aren't that different from Justin. While he may have been spoiled and overly demanding of his parents, he did something that we are prone to do more often than we realize; he completely missed the gift his father wanted to give him because it wasn't packaged in the way he thought it would be. Even though he was expecting a blessing on that fateful graduation day, he wasn't able to accept it when it was right in the palm of his hand, because he had another expectation so clearly etched in his mind. As a result, he tossed the gift aside without acknowledgment or thanks.

As you begin to live with the power of positive expectation, keep Justin's story in mind as a warning. Expect God to bless you, but be careful about expecting that blessing to come in the exact way you think it will or should. God's gifts manifest themselves in our lives in many forms. We need to be aware of the various ways he may bless us, so that when he does we can recognize the blessing and acknowledge him as the source.

Four Types of Blessings

There are four primary ways God gives back to us when we serve others. He blesses us through tangible blessings, intangible blessings, greater influence, and visible miracles. Let's look at each one of these in more detail.

Tangible Blessings: Tangible blessings are God's most obvious blessings. Usually financial, these blessings can come in the form of increased pay, an unexpected check, having a material need met, receiving a free meal or new clothes, etc. The list could go on and on, but you get the idea. Tangible blessings are just that—tangible. You can see and touch them.

Not long ago, The Journey was doing a Christmas offering to raise money for the ministry initiatives God was leading us into for the next year. A woman in our church who was struggling financially decided to take a step of faith and give $120 to the offering. With this gift she was blessing all of the people who would be touched by the initiatives that the offering was going to support, including international missionaries and children in our city, to name a few. Later she told me that a week and a half after she gave that $120, she received a $120 Christmas bonus from her boss completely out of the blue. Her story isn't unique. Time and time again, God proves himself faithful to give tangible blessings back to people who honor him with their finances.

Here's the key: this woman was walking in positive expectation, so when her boss handed her a bonus check, she immediately recognized it as a gift from God. Through this experience God drew her closer to himself and made her want to bless others even more. You can never outgive

God. Don't give to receive, but know that if you give with the right heart God is going to bless you in return.

Intangible Blessings: Sometimes you will bless another person and, rather than being blessed tangibly, you will get an intangible blessing in return. God loves to fill our lives with intangible blessings. We should live in positive expectation of them and be quick to embrace every one that comes our way. He blesses us with love, health, sound mind, a sense of purpose, friendships, his presence, peace, and comfort, just to name a few; the list is endless. God's intangible blessings are not always considered as much fun or as coveted as his tangible blessings, but they are the ones that truly lead to joy.

Have you ever noticed that when you serve someone, it makes you feel good? That's an intangible blessing, in and of itself. God etched this sense of fulfillment that comes from being a servant into your DNA. The substance of The Greatness Principle is part of your being; when you live it out, you get the intangible blessing of knowing that you are partnering with God in his work. What could be more meaningful or significant than that?

I like to tell the story of a high-powered investment broker who attended The Journey regularly. This guy, Stuart, was as sharp as they come. He was smart and engaging. He lived in a beautiful apartment on the Upper West Side of Manhattan. He traveled internationally for work, stayed in five-star hotels, and dined with CEOs and CFOs of major corporations. Still, whenever Stuart was in town on a Thursday night, he would show up at The Journey offices for what we call Super Service Thursday—a time when volunteers come in for an hour to fold and stuff programs and take care of other tasks that need to be handled for that weekend's worship services.

One Thursday night, a young pastor on our staff struck up a conversation with Stuart, during which he thanked Stuart for being there. Stuart replied with, "Oh, I would hate to miss it. This hour on Thursday night is the best hour of my week. It's one of the only times I really feel satisfied and happy with what I'm doing." Stuart had a glamorous, well-paying dream job, but he understood that his job didn't bring him ultimate significance. Rather, serving God through serving the church brought him the intangible blessing of knowing he was doing something that mattered for eternity.

Greater Influence: At the end of chapter 4, I mentioned our call to shine in a way that reflects God's glory.

> It is one of the most beautiful compensations of life that no man can sincerely try to help another without helping himself.
>
> Ralph Waldo Emerson

Take a look at Matthew's words again, within the larger context:

> You are the light of the world—like a city on a hilltop that cannot be hidden. No one lights a lamp and then puts it under a basket. Instead, a lamp is placed on a stand, where it gives light to everyone in the house. In the same way, let your good deeds shine out for all to see, so that everyone will praise your heavenly Father. (Matt. 5:14–16)

As a Christ follower you have been positioned and commanded to bring God's light into the world. He wants your light to make a difference. In other words, God wants you to have influence on the world around you—influence that points people back toward his truth. When you serve him well, greater influence may be one of the ways he blesses you.

Perhaps you decide to take a step of faith and bless others in a small way. Let's say your church has small groups and you want to serve by hosting a group—that is, by simply opening up your home as a meeting place. God may eventually bless you by turning that small step of service into greater opportunity by calling you to be a small group leader. Later, he may call you to even greater opportunity by placing you in a higher position of leadership within your church's small group structure. Of course, this doesn't always happen—and you certainly need to be sensitive to his guidance—but sometimes God gives you more occasions to shine your light the more you shine it.

Visible Miracles: Visible miracles are an incredible blessing; they are actually my favorite type. A visible miracle is when God gives you the opportunity to see him do a miracle firsthand through your willingness to serve. Sometimes visible miracles are small. Maybe you grab coffee with a friend who is facing a hard situation, and through your encouraging words you see his whole countenance change. Or perhaps you know of a family who is struggling to put food on the table, so you decide to take them a meal—and you get to see the pure joy on the youngest child's face when she realizes that they are going to have such a nice dinner. Those are small visible miracles. They are your chance to see God working through you.

Some visible miracles are a little more distant. Say you decide to give money to a new ministry that's starting in the next state. Later, when you hear a report of how many people that ministry has been able to reach for Jesus, you get to see the result of something you took a direct part in through your support. That's a visible miracle. When God gives you the opportunity to witness visible miracles, you have the awesome privilege of seeing exactly how you are partnering with him in accomplishing his purposes in the world.

The power of positive expectation and the acknowledged blessing that comes from it quickly become cyclical. As you bless others, God blesses you. You receive that blessing and thank him for it. As a result, you are drawn closer to God and begin to serve him even more. In response, he blesses you more. You recognize the blessing, thank him for it, are drawn closer to him, and want to serve him at yet a higher level. Then he blesses you at an even higher level. See how this goes? Through being a blessing and being blessed, you will quickly become part of an upward spiral of meaning, purpose, and significance. You will become great.

Glance back at the definition of positive expectation in this chapter. With this in mind, how can you begin to incorporate positive expectation into your everyday life?

_____

_____

_____

How have you seen God bless you in tangible ways?

_____

_____

_____

In intangible ways?

_____

_____

_____

With greater influence?

_____

_____

_____

Through visible miracles?

_____

_____

_____

6

the heart of greatness

In the poor man who knocks at my door, in my ailing
mother, in the young man who seeks my advice, the
Lord himself is present.

C. S. Lewis

In the early 1970s, Princeton University conducted
a study that got to the heart of good intentions. The
experiment involved students at Princeton's Theological
Seminary—people who were preparing to go out into
the world as Christian leaders. These were young men
and women who studied every word Jesus said. They
knew where he stood on service. They knew how he defined greatness. What was going to be expected of them

should have been a no-brainer. But, as the study ended up proving, all the knowledge in the world is useless if you don't take the time to apply it.

Based on one of Jesus's most often retold parables, the now infamous Princeton study has come to be known as The Good Samaritan Study. Interestingly, Jesus presents this parable as part of an answer to questioning about how to be in right standing with God. And he uses it to illustrate something central to our ability to authentically and continuously live by The Greatness Principle—love. Let's take a look at the Q&A session that precedes the actual parable:

> One day an expert in religious law stood up to test Jesus by asking him this question: "Teacher, what should I do to inherit eternal life?" Jesus replied, "What does the law of Moses say? How do you read it?" The man answered, "'You must love the Lord your God with all your heart, all your soul, all your strength, and all your mind.' And, 'Love your neighbor as yourself.'" "Right!" Jesus told him. "Do this and you will live!" (Luke 10:25–28)

We've established that you and I are to think and act like Jesus, which means following his example of service to others. We've got that. But what is the heart of servanthood? Well, there's a hint in the question itself.

Love is at the core of authentic service. In Matthew's account of Jesus's exchange with the expert in religious law, Jesus says that the two commands mentioned—to love God and to love your neighbor as yourself—are the two most important commandments in all of Scripture.

These two commands, and the way they interact with each other, give us a glimpse at the very life force of

---

Love is at the core of authentic service.

---

service. When we love God with all of our heart, soul, strength, and mind, we want to serve him out of that love. The way we do that is by taking on Jesus's countenance and blessing others. Through our partnership with God and our deference to him, we are able to fulfill the second command and truly love our neighbor as ourselves. Remember C. S. Lewis's insight from chapter 3? The ability to love our neighbor manifests through our obedience to God. So as we obey more and more—and as our love continues to grow—we are increasingly willing and able to serve those around us from a pure heart.

Now, let's take a look at how the parable of the Good Samaritan ties in:

> The man wanted to justify his actions, so he asked Jesus, "And who is my neighbor?" Jesus replied with

a story: "A Jewish man was traveling from Jerusalem down to Jericho, and he was attacked by bandits. They stripped him of his clothes, beat him up, and left him half dead beside the road. By chance a priest came along. But when he saw the man lying there, he crossed to the other side of the road and passed him by. A Temple assistant walked over and looked at him lying there, but he also passed by on the other side. Then a despised Samaritan came along, and when he saw the man, he felt compassion for him. Going over to him, the Samaritan soothed his wounds with olive oil and wine and bandaged them. Then he put the man on his own donkey and took him to an inn, where he took care of him. The next day he handed the innkeeper two silver coins, telling him, 'Take care of this man. If his bill runs higher than this, I'll pay you the next time I'm here.' Now which of these three would you say was a neighbor to the man who was attacked by bandits?" Jesus asked. The man replied, "The one who showed him mercy." Then Jesus said, "Yes, now go and do the same." (Luke 10:29–37)

Through this parable Jesus uses the example of the Samaritan to remind us of our responsibility to serve when we see need, and to make the point that the needy people we see are our neighbors whom we are called to love. Take another look at the verse we examined in chapter 3:

> Do not withhold good from those who deserve it when it's in your power to help them. If you can help your neighbor now, don't say, "Come back tomorrow, and then I'll help you." (Prov. 3:27–28)

Consider Paul's words in Philippians 2:4 one more time too:

> Don't look out only for your own interests, but take an interest in others, too.

The priest and the temple assistant who walked by the battered man were not only looking out for their own interests; they were also withholding good from someone who desperately needed it. These two were religious leaders. They knew exactly what they should do, but they let excuses keep them from doing it. They crossed to the other side of the road and kept walking.

The Samaritan, on the other hand, had compassion on the man in need. Considering his own needs secondary to the urgent need he saw in front of him, he inconvenienced himself to take care of the one God had put in his path. The Scripture actually says that the Good Samaritan showed the beaten and bruised man mercy. Again, mercy is literally *love in action*.

Modern-Day Mercy

Let's get back to the Princeton study. Wanting to test what modern-day seminary students would do if they came face-to-face with their own Good Samaritan situation, some prominent researchers crafted a plan and identified a few dozen unaware seminary students as their guinea pigs. They called the subjects into their office one by one and told each that he or she had just been chosen to give an impromptu talk in the recording studio in the next building over.

Half of the students were given the parable of the Good Samaritan as their topic. The rest were assigned different, random topics. Then they were given one of three senses of urgency: some of the students were told they were already late and that they should hurry over to the recording studio; some were told that they had just enough time to get there; and some were told that that they had a little time to spare before they would have to give their talk.

The researchers hired an actor to play the role of a man in need and planted him in a prominent spot along the sidewalk that each of the students would be taking to get to the recording studio. He was disheveled, slumped over, and looked like he had been the victim of a heart attack or something similar. They wanted to find out which of the students would stop to help the hurting man and which ones would walk right by him.

Here's what they found: being pressed for time had a major impact on whether or not the students stopped and showed concern. Sixty-three percent of those who had been told they had some extra time stopped; 45 percent of those who thought they had just enough time stopped; only 10 percent of the students who thought they were already late stopped. Gender, age, race, and religious denomination made no difference. Neither did their speech topic—the people who had the Good Samaritan parable in mind as they walked by were no more likely to stop if they were in a hurry than those who didn't.[1]

When I first learned about this study, I tried to put myself in the situation of each of these students. What would I have done under the same circumstances? What would you have done? Would your immediate concerns have been more important than helping someone who was obviously in a desperate situation? The man on the street would have qualified as our neighbor; we are commanded to love him. Walking by him without showing mercy doesn't indicate much love. Here's another way to think about it: What if you were the one who found yourself slumped over on the sidewalk? How would you want passersby to respond to you?

In both Jesus's parable of the Good Samaritan and in The Good Samaritan Study, love is the ultimate difference maker. It would have been impossible for any of the students to feel love for the needy person in front of them and yet still ignore him. At that moment, self-interest crowded out selfless love. The students who didn't stop were simply modern-day examples of the priest and temple assistant from the parable. They didn't want to risk the consequences of being late for their appointment, whereas the good Samaritans were more concerned for another person's well-being than their own. Martin Luther King put this in perspective well when, speaking on Jesus's parable, he said:

> The first question which the priest and the Levite asked was, "If I stop to help this man, what will happen to me?" But . . . the Good Samaritan reversed the question, "If I do not stop to help this man, what will happen to him?"[2]

Paul tells us in 1 Corinthians 13 that love is patient, kind, and does not seek its own way. Love is selfless. And as the Good Samaritan in Jesus's parable and the Samaritans in the study show, love never fails to help a neighbor in need.

Along with using this parable to make a point about love, Jesus also answers his inquisitor's question about who constitutes a neighbor. In short, Jesus is saying that your neighbors are all around you. They are the people

> What does love look like? It has the hands to help others. It has the feet to hasten to the poor and needy. It has eyes to see misery and want. It has the ears to hear the sighs and sorrows of men. That is what love looks like.
>
> Saint Augustine

closest to you, of course, but they are also the unexpected ones who cross your path. Your neighbor is anyone God puts in front of you with an immediate need or anyone he guides you to bless on a larger scale.

Do You Know Your Neighbors?

You and I may not pass bandit victims or someone facing a major medical emergency very often, but we do come into contact with people we are called to love all the time. By embracing The Greatness Principle, you have the opportunity to be the Good Samaritan in the lives of those God puts in your path. You can emanate mercy by being quick to show your neighbors love in action. Here are just a few of your neighbors that Jesus wants you to recognize as such and love:

Family: Greatness starts at home. Wouldn't it be wonderful to live in a family where everyone is loving each other as much as they love themselves and blessing each other every chance they get? You can be the catalyst by deciding to live out The Greatness Principle at home first. As you recognize your family members' needs and bless them accordingly, God will bless you with stronger relationships and more peace in your home. Not to mention, your family members will likely start to follow your lead and serve each other as well. We'll discuss some specific ways you can begin serving your family in chapter 7.

Friends: Whether you realize it or not, your example has tremendous influence on your friends. When they recognize that you are intentionally blessing them, the dynamic of the relationship will be changed for the better. Since friends tend to emulate one another, they will probably begin blessing you in return, which will direct them toward the power of The Greatness Principle by default.

Undoubtedly, you have some friends who are Christians and some who aren't. The best way you can bless both is simply by being aware of their needs and proactively taking steps to meet those needs. In addition, one of the greatest ways to bless your nonbelieving friends is to give them an opportunity to meet Jesus by inviting them to church with you. We'll discuss the importance of this invitation in more detail in chapter 7.

Church: If you aren't part of a local Christ-centered church, let me encourage you to seek one out and get connected. You'll find like-minded believers you can relate to and biblical leadership to encourage you in your faith. Not to mention, the church is one of the best places to apply The Greatness Principle through serving others. You will discover opportunities to get involved in ways that suit your passions and gifting, whether that's singing on the worship team, leading a small group, working in the parking lot, or encouraging children and youth. (For a free tool to help you find a church in your area, visit www.TheGreatnessPrinciple.com.)

If you are part of a healthy church but you've been sitting on the sidelines when it comes to service, let this be the nudge that causes you to get involved. Now that you understand the joy, fulfillment, and purpose that comes with stepping out of your comfort zone and being a blessing, you have no reason to wait. Find out what ministries your church has that you feel most drawn to participate in and then step up and be great.

Community/City/World: You have neighbors who are in desperate need of blessing in your immediate community, in your greater city, and across the globe. Resist the natural urge to be so consumed with your own little corner of the world that you fail to recognize your place in the bigger picture. Who is God leading you to bless in your community? How about in your city? What international needs touch your heart?

Remember to be sensitive to God's leading as you pursue opportunities to serve on a larger scale. Consider your passions. Maybe you feel drawn to work with children in Africa who have been orphaned by AIDS, to feed the hungry in the next neighborhood, to build houses for the poor in your town, or to visit with the lonely and sick on your street. Once you feel guided to bless your community, city, or world in a specific way, check first with your local church to see if they have any ministries that are in line with your desires. If not, begin looking into nonprofit organizations that focus where you are interested. (For a list of recommended service organizations, visit www.TheGreatnessPrinciple.com.)

When you live out The Greatness Principle by blessing your neighbors from a heart of love, you model the greatness of God to a watching world. Consider what Bishop Kallistos Ware once said: "We become truly personal by loving God and by loving other humans. . . . In its deepest sense, love is the life, the energy, of the Creator in us."[3] Our job is to exude that love, to express it in a practical way by stopping and caring for the needs we see as we make our journey down the road of life.

Who could you be more intentional about showing love to . . .
In your family:

_____

_____

_____

Among your friends:

_____

_____

_____

In your church:

_____

_____

_____

Throughout your community/city/world:

_____

_____

_____

7

making the list

Greatness is not found in possessions, power, position or prestige. It is discovered in goodness, humility, service and character.

William Arthur Ward

I have to confess something. I don't usually read *Forbes* magazine, but I can't keep myself from picking up the yearly edition where they announce their roll of billionaires. I like to check whether or not I made the list. I know it may surprise you, but I have yet to see my name alongside Bill Gates and Warren Buffet. Before I became a Christian, I used to think that making the *Forbes* list was the ultimate sign of greatness. But, as we've discovered in these pages, God defines greatness quite differently. Just because the people on that list are great in the world's eyes doesn't mean they are great in God's. Then again, they may be; but if they are, it has nothing to do with their financial success and everything to do with their willingness to humble themselves in service.

The good news for you and me is that we don't have to be on the *Forbes* list to be great. (Making the cut would just be a bonus!) We can wake up every single morning and be extraordinary. We can go to bed every night knowing that we are partnering with God to make a difference in the world. That's what I call "everyday greatness." Though it may not get us written up in a magazine, it's the most significant way we can use our lives. We will be great in God's eyes, a blessing to the people around us and blessed abundantly in return.

Everyday Greatness

Now that The Greatness Principle is fully ingrained into your consciousness, I want to give you some practical ways that you can start blessing the people in your world right away. Remember, The Greatness Principle is not theory. It is foundational, biblical truth, and it will manifest blessing in the lives of others and in your own life as you commit to living it out. Here are seven ways to get started:

1. *Encourage the people around you.* Encouraging someone with your words is one of the simplest, yet most powerful ways you can be a blessing. As Paul writes in Ephesians 4:29, "Don't use foul or abusive language. Let everything you say be good and helpful, so that your words will be an encouragement to those who hear them." Here are a few practical ways you can use your words to serve those around you:

   - Pay your co-worker a sincere compliment.
   - Congratulate your child on a job well done.
   - Listen to a friend who needs to talk and respond thoughtfully.
   - Intentionally build up your spouse.

2. *Help someone in need.* You'll begin seeing immediate ways to help people in need as you start practicing awareness. When you do, don't cross to the other side of the road. Be willing to humble and inconvenience yourself in order to lift someone else up. As my friend Steve Sjogren says, "Small things done with great love will change the world."

> How wonderful is it that nobody need wait a single moment before starting to improve the world.
>
> Anne Frank

Helping others is contagious. By simply being quick to lend a hand to someone in need, you could spark a revolution. When someone sees you offering help, he or she is likely to do the same when the opportunity presents itself. Imagine the difference we could make if we all decided to help another person every day. Here are a few practical ways you can help the people around you:

- Carry an elderly woman's groceries to her car.
- Help a mom lift her stroller up a flight of stairs.
- Take a meal to a family who is going through a difficult time.
- Offer to babysit for a friend who has young children.
- The possibilities are endless—have open eyes and help where you can!

3. *Invite your friends to church.* Inviting your friends who don't know Jesus to church is a great act of service. While it takes a good dose of humility

on your part, extending that invitation goes far beyond simply encouraging and helping in the grand scheme of blessing others. I know it's much easier to invite your friends to a ball game or out to dinner than it is to invite them to come to church with you, but push through the intimidation and take that step of faith.

Here's some news that might make things a little easier: statistics show that you are actually risking very little when you invite your friends to church. Around 50 percent of your unchurched friends will come with you the first time you ask. That percentage goes up substantially with a second, third, or fourth invitation. Believe me, you will not offend any of your friends by inviting them to church. Even if they say no, they will be touched that you cared enough to ask. And just think of what could happen if they say yes.

Colossians 4:5 tells us, "Live wisely among those who are not believers, and make the most of every opportunity." When you seize an opportunity to invite your friends to church, you are inviting them to a place where they can learn about their Creator and have their deepest needs met. What better way could there be to bless your friends than that?

4. *Connect with your family.* As I mentioned in chapter 6, greatness starts at home. Even though we may have the best of intentions for keeping our family members at the top of our priority list, all too often they slip toward the bottom when things get busy. We need to be intentional about blessing our family members every chance we get.

God considers honoring your relationship with your family so important that he addresses it in the Ten Commandments. In Exodus 20:12, he says, "Honor your father and mother. Then you will live a long, full life in the land the LORD your God is giving you." The first four of the Ten Commandments are about your relationship with God; the next six are about your relationships with other people. Interestingly, this one is the fifth commandment, which makes it the very first thing God addresses in the relational category. Not to mention, it is the only commandment that has a promise attached to it. God promises that if you honor your parents, you will live a long, full life.

While this commandment focuses specifically on honoring your mother and father, the point also applies to your spouse, children, brothers, sisters, and extended family. Our willingness to proactively bless our family members will create stronger family ties and be a great example to the rest of the world. Here are a few practical ways you can connect with your family right away:

- Schedule a date night with your spouse.
- Spend some one-on-one time with each of your kids.
- Call your parents.
- Plan a trip to visit your extended family.

5. *Pray for your friends.* Praying for your friends is a mighty way to bless them. As James tells us, "The earnest prayer of a righteous person has great power and produces wonderful results" (James 5:16). When you see a need in your friend's life, praying about it may be the most helpful thing you can do. Pray and act; but even when you can't act, always pray. Prayers truly make a difference. Here are a few ways you can start praying for your friends today:

- Pray that they will come to know Jesus, if they don't already.
- Pray that they will be sensitive to God's leading in their life.
- Pray for their health and safety.
- Pray that they will be a strong witness for God.

6. *Serve your city or town.* Perhaps you've never thought about it much, but God has you living where you are for a specific reason. He wants you to impact your city or town in the unique way that only you can. Consider what Jeremiah writes: "Work for the peace and prosperity of the city where I sent you. . . . Pray to the LORD for it, for its welfare will determine your welfare" (Jer. 29:7).

As we've discussed, you and I are called to be a light—to shine in a way that reflects God's glory for all to see. What we do in a church service or as a community of believers has little influence if we don't step out and engage the area we call home. Bless your city or town by showing its inhabitants the gospel of Jesus Christ in action. Here are a few practical ways you can get started:

- Get involved with your church's community outreach ministries.
- Serve at a local homeless shelter.
- Sign up to build houses with Habitat for Humanity.
- Tutor children in low-income areas.
- Say thank you to your local police officers and firefighters.

- Again, the possibilities are endless—just look around you.

7. *Attend your church.* This one may surprise you, but attending church is critical to your ability to apply The Greatness Principle long term. Left to our own devices, we get lazy about serving others. Over time, selfishness creeps back in and we forget to shift our focus outward. Going to church keeps truth in front of us and encouragement around us, so we don't slip away from embracing God's best for our lives. As Scripture advises us, "Let us not neglect our meeting together, as some people do, but encourage one another, especially now that the day of his return is drawing near" (Heb. 10:25).

Whether you ever make the *Forbes* billionaire list, you can make the list of people who are mightily used by God to accomplish his purposes in this world. You can join the ranks of those greats who have focused their lives around a guiding principle and have found meaning and purpose in the process. You can be the one who shines the light of a great God for all to see as you glorify him by blessing others with excellence. When our limited time on earth is compared with the eternity we'll spend with God in heaven, it's easy to see which lists actually matter.

I almost forgot. There's one more way God blesses you when you bless others; he blesses you with treasures in heaven. Jesus tells us in Matthew:

> Don't store up treasures here on earth, where moths eat them and rust destroys them, and where thieves break in and steal. Store your treasures in heaven, where moths and rust cannot destroy, and thieves do not break in and steal. (Matt. 6:19–20)

When the day comes—and it will come—that your obituary runs in your local newspaper, all of the money, toys, accolades, power, and prestige that you gained on this earth will mean nothing. As far as you're concerned, they'll be gone. Only two things will remain—what you poured into other people, and the blessings that God will be continuing to pour out on you in return.

What is one thing you will do today or tomorrow to live out The Greatness Principle?

_____

_____

_____

notes

Chapter 1 Discovering True Greatness

1. "Excerpt from the Will of Alfred Nobel," Nobelprize.org, accessed February 29, 2012, http://www.nobelprize.org/alfred_nobel/will/short_testamente.html.

2. Stephen R. Covey, *The Seven Habits of Highly Effective People* (New York: Simon & Schuster, 1989), 98.

3. Winston Churchill, "Never Give In," Welcome to Winston Churchill, accessed February 29, 2012, http://www.winstonchurchill.org/learn/speeches/speeches-of-winston-churchill/103-never-give-in.

Chapter 2 Recognizing Great Opportunities

1. Rick Warren, *The Purpose Driven Life: What on Earth Am I Here For?* (Grand Rapids: Zondervan, 2002), 17.

2. "Hunger In America," Feeding America, accessed February 29, 2012, http://feedingamerica.org/hunger-in-america.aspx.

3. Give A Drop, accessed February 29, 2012, http://www.giveadrop.com/.

Chapter 3 Seizing Significance

1. C. S. Lewis, *Mere Christianity* (London: Collins, 1956), 87.

Chapter 4 Credit Where Credit Is Due

1. Lynne Hybels and Bill Hybels, *Rediscovering Church: The Story and Vision of Willow Creek Community Church* (Grand Rapids: Zondervan, 1995), 192.

Chapter 6 The Heart of Greatness

1. "Moral Philosophy Meets Social Psychology," Princeton.edu, February 29, 2012, http://www.princeton.edu/~harman/Papers/Virtue.html.

2. Donald T. Phillips, *Martin Luther King, Jr., on Leadership: Inspiration and Wisdom for Challenging Times* (New York: Warner, 2000), 296.

3. Kallistos Ware, Beliefnet.com, accessed April 27, 2012, www.beliefnet.com/Quotes/Christian/K/Kallistos-Ware/we-become-truly-personal-by-loving-god-and-by-lovi.aspx.

acknowledgments

Nelson Searcy: My thanks to Jesus Christ for the opportunity to serve him, his church, and his kingdom—may I truly be great in your eyes. I also would like to thank each of these individuals for their contributions to this book: Kelley Searcy, Alexander Searcy, Jennifer Dykes Henson, Kerrick Thomas, Jason Haltey, Scott Whitaker, Tommy Duke, Jimmy Britt, Chad Allen, and all the pastors, writers, and teachers who have influenced my understanding of biblical servanthood.

Jennifer Dykes Henson: Thanks first to God for giving us such clear direction on how to achieve true greatness in our lives. Thanks to Nelson Searcy for inviting me into this incredible work. And thanks also to my mom, Sandra Dykes, and to my husband, Brian Henson—you have both taught me much about greatness in the way you model selfless service each and every day.

Nelson Searcy is the founding lead pastor of The Journey Church of the City with locations in New York City, Queens, Brooklyn, and Boca Raton, FL. He is also the founder of www.ChurchLeaderInsights.com. He and his church appear routinely on lists such as the 50 Most Influential Churches and the 25 Most Innovative Leaders.

Jennifer Dykes Henson is a freelance writer based in New York City. She has served as a writer/producer and ministry consultant to organizations across the East Coast. Jennifer also worked with Dr. Charles Stanley as the manager of marketing communications for In Touch Ministries in Atlanta, Georgia.

More from Nelson Searcy

Taking a comprehensive approach to the often frustrating issue of finding and retaining volunteers, *Connect* gives leaders the practical insight and tools they need to effectively involve people in serving the local church.

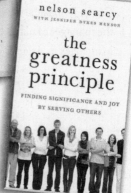

This little book packs a wealth of practical insight and inspired ideas that will energize church members to volunteer their time and talents. Perfect for small groups!

An Attitude of Worship

For Church Members

With *Revolve*, readers will see that when they approach worship with a "what can I get out of this" attitude, they're bound to be disappointed. However, worshiping God as a way of life not only honors God but also satisfies our souls. Built-in action steps at the end of each short chapter will give readers specific ideas about how to refocus their attention on God and live each day in an attitude of worship.

For Worship Leaders

Engage, the church leaders' companion to *Revolve*, is a step-by-step, stress-free guide to planning worship services that allow for and foster true life change.

How to Handle Your Finances in a Godly Manner

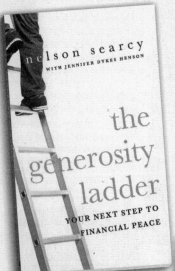

Published alongside *Maximize* is Searcy's book *The Generosity Ladder*, for anyone who desires to handle money with excellence. Written to answer all of the questions and misunderstandings that surround the intersection of God and money, *The Generosity Ladder* will allow laypeople to fully grasp God's plan for their finances.

Maximize is the ultimate how-to book for pastors and church leaders who long for their churches to be fully resourced and able to carry out ministry initiatives without financial strain. Shining a light on the often taboo subject of money, *Maximize* offers an innovative, step-by-step plan for systemizing and maximizing financial gifts while growing strong disciples.